HEALING

AN

AILING

UNITED STATES

FEDERAL GOVERNMENT

MELVIN S. ROSH, MD

LEARN AS YOU WERE TO
LIVE FOREVER
LIVE AS YOU WERE TO
DIE TOMORROW.

MAHATMA GANDHI

DEDICATED TO MY
LOVING WIFE,
CHILDREN AND
GRANDCHILDREN

AND TO ALL

WHO CHERISH
AMERICA

CONTENTS

Dedication.......................................5

Introduction......................................7

chapter 1- Acute & Chronic Treatment....13

Chapter 2 – Mastering Life Skills.............18

Chapter 3 - Funding Elections..................28

chapter 4 - Politician Campaigning.........34

chapter 5 –Term Limits.........................42

chapter 6 – Money, Money, Money.........48

chapter 7 -Federal Taxes.......................59

chapter 8 – Federal Holidays...................72

Chapter 9 – Federal Voting.....................78

chapter 10 – Economic Upheavals...........81

chapter 11 – Student Loan......................96

chapter 12 – Responsibility....................102

Chaprer 13 – Evaliatng the Truth...........107

chapter 14 – Greatness of America........109

About the author..................................119

Introduction

The book, "Healing an Ailing United States Federal Government", is a natural sequel to a previous book, "A Medical Doc's Prescription to Heal an Ailing America". This treatise discusses topics that have not previously been touched upon, and mainly focuses on problems that the United States Federal Government faces today, giving suggested solving solutions

America is one the greatest countries that the world has ever known, but that does not mean that it is perfect. There are many areas that can and should be improved to make life for all its citizens more pleasant, more humane, and more rewarding.

Throughout the history of the world, nations have always been endowed with a very small group of wealthy, prominent individuals that were able to accumulate great fortunes, and control the direction of a country; a middle class group of individuals that supported the smaller wealthier group of leaders, and a very large lower class   that had to struggle to survive. The wealthiest group, many times, represented less than one percent of the total population. This   observation applies to present day twenty-first century America, as well.

Over the coarse of time, humankind has experimented with many different forms of governments. Some have lasted a short period of time before being overturned; other have lasted for centuries.   Societies have been led by absolute rulers, such as Pharaohs, Emperors, Kings, Czars, Dictators or leaders of Totalitarian or Autocratic states, and others have tried governments controlled by the populace, such as republics or democracies.

Some cultures lasted for centuries, others just decades. But in each culture, a similar distribution of wealth existed. In primitive cultures, fortune was determined by quantity of land, or number of animals, such as goats, cows, or camels, that comprised the flocks that were owned. As money came into existence, wealth was measured in the amount of currency that an individual possessed. But in spite of how wealth was calculated, the same   three divisions of societies that were previously described existed in all the different types of governments.

In modern times, The United States of America has become a beacon of democracy among the nations of the world; a country that, over time, has given most of its citizens a voice to vote, and the ability to choose those who lead them.

America has not arrived at this point easily. Fortunately, the Founders of the Country were wise to provide a guiding document that could be altered, and one that could be adapted to accommodate the needs of future events Many wrongs, that were present at the onset of the founding of the Country, were incorporated into its original Constitution, but with time these wrongs, such as slavery or gender discrimination, are being corrected. Much more still has to be done.

Over the two hundred and fifty years, America has been labeled as a republic, and frequently mislabeled, a democracy. A republic is a form of government in which supreme power rests with its citizens to vote for representatives, who in turn, are to exercise the wishes of their electorate. A democracy is defined as a government in which power is controlled by the people, themselves, such as exhibited by the male citizenry of Ancient Athens. Athenian women and slaves had no say in their government.

Scholars tend to label countries by their type of governing pattern, such as democracy, Constitutional Monarchy, socialism, and so forth. Some politicians in America use these labels to scare their constituents to vote a particular way. For example, Senator McCarthy, using Senatorial hearings in the 1950s, ruined many lives by insinuating they were Communist. America should not be troubled by labels. The laws of the United States should reflect what is best for the country, whether the idea originates from socialistic, communistic, democratic or conservative philosophies.

America is a republic, founded by a group of men, who like Ancient Athens, formed a government which did not apply to women or slaves. The founding fathers of America designed a government of Representatives to be controlled by its male wealthy citizens.

America was supposed to be a "land of the brave and free"; but, unfortunately, many times, has exhibited a "land of greed and selfishness". The robber barons of the nineteenth century used unethical practices to accumulate wealth. In the late twentieth century, the "me-too" generation saw the rise of individuality; degrading the concept of group cooperation. These individuals favored their own agenda, irrespective of the majority's opinions or the greater good.

"My Way of No Way" is the war cry of many politicians today. Compromise does not seem to be an option. America has a wedge tearing it apart. However, this is not the first time in American history that the country has been divided.

The book, "A Medical Doc's Prescription to Healing of America" deals with a potpourri of subjects, such as medical practice in America, malpractice, big pharma, discrimination, climate control, immigration, gun control, abortion, antisemitism, economic slavery, the LGBTQ community, female subjugation, and other important issues that require political correction. This book, "Healing an Ailing United States Federal Government", deals with different subjects, but, both books are formatted to suggest acute and chronic therapies to make our great nation stronger, and strive for values that are consistent with the "American Way of Life".

This book, "Healing an Ailing United States Federal Government", concentrates on the Central Federal Government and does not propose, at any time, to addresses problems of State Governments, even though, some of the cures suggested may be applicable to some States.

The major topics touched upon include funding of elections, political campaigning, term limits for office holders, federal taxation, inflation and recession, student loans, and other important subjects that effect every American.

CHAPTER I

ACUTE AND CHRONIC TREATMENTS

An Approach to Healing America

Modern medicine attempts to be as scientific as possible. Double blind studies are performed to discover the true nature of diseases and to find a cure for the malady. When possible and feasible, laboratory animals, to the chagrin of animal lovers, have been used to try to expose and treat the root causes of human diseases.

But, the practice of medicine is just as much an art as it is a science. From the onset of humankind, every culture has had its "medicine man"; a person respected by people to heal them of their afflictions. Primitive and some modern cultures use herbs and plants to cure their sick. Ancient cultures of China, Egypt, Babylonia, and India, all developed different sophisticated ways to treat   sicknesses. In the fifth century BCE, Hippocrates laid down a set of ethical rules to be followed when treating a sick individual. Physicians of Western Medicine take this oath in   which they solemnly   swear   not to do harm to the patients they treat.

Physicians practice the best type of medicine that they know. At first, there were no medical schools. The knowledge of medical techniques was passed down   through apprenticeships,   and   each   mentor   had developed a specific way of handling patients, depending on the   training and expertise of the individual.

The practice of Medicine has changed over time, as different ways of treatments have taken hold. George Washington, our first President of this great nation, was treated by eminent physicians of the time. Having pneumonia, Washington's physician bled him several   times.   Bleeding,   known   as phlebotomy, was   a very popular curative procedure for over three thousand years and can be traced back to the ancient cultures of Egypt, Greeks and Romans.

Not showing any improvement, the doctors of

George Washington consulted with a specialist, who recommended additional bleeding. The patient died of pneumonia. Unfortunately, the excessive bleeding contributed to the demise of the first President of the United States.

In approaching a patient, a doctor must listen to the patient, determine what facts presented by the patient are relevant, and render the best treatment, in the doctor's opinion, for the disease.

Usually most diseases have an acute and chronic phase, and different treatments may be needed for each stage. For example, a child develops a Streptococcal sore throat and a physician treats the patient with an antibiotic. This is the acute phase. Several weeks later, Rheumatic heart symptoms are noted, a chronic stage, and a different treatment has to be instituted.

A similar approach can be adapted to curing many problems that an ailing America is presently facing. Treating with measures that are appropriate for an acute phase may not be suitable for chronic situations, so that, a different approach may be necessary.

Another important factor in healing America is to have an educated populace, who can distinguish truth from falsehood, will be willing to compromise, and who will be faithful to the country, and not to a small group who will do anything to obtain goals, that favors themselves and not the country.

But a knowledgeable populace doesn't just occur naturally. People have to be educated in how to recognize the truth and to recognize when situations of danger appear.

Teaching our children to appreciate a country that is just and fair; one without prejudice and hatred; one that provides the necessary needs to achieve a healthy and cohesive society, as well as instilling love of one's country is important, if America is to be great, and more, importantly, to survive.

The family would be the ideal institution to impart important information of managing life's skills to the next generation, and should certainly be encouraged to do so. However, many families are unable to be the major source to instruct their children in life's skills. Some parents have no time, being burdened with making a living. Some must have more than one job to survive. Other families are actually too "toxic" to demonstrate role model behavior. One or both parents may be under the influence of alcohol or other addicting substances, and, unfortunately, too many families exhibit abusive behavior.

Therefore, the major burden of teaching life mastering skills to future generations falls upon school systems to fill the void. Some school districts are instituting this form of instruction at the present time, under the title, "Social and Emotional Learning Program", which will be discussed in the next chapter in more detail.

The reader may wonder why there is a chapter concerning medical approaches to solving problems concerning the health of individuals. The topics involving medicine and politics may be very different, but the approach to solving a cure for diseases or political problems is similar. In both cases, optimal outcomes are desirable, and like medicine, political solutions will change with time.

Chapter 2

MASTERING LIFE'S SKILLS

(Social and Emotional Learning Program)

America is not adequately preparing children against possible future dangers, such as addiction, bullying, gun violence, prejudice, sexual molestation and many other potential calamities. Children are also not being prepared to handle many other life situations, such as relationships with friends or significant others, personal care and self esteem, nor are many being instilled with pride and knowledge of the American form of government.

Millions of Americas become addicted to dangerous chemicals, of which, over eighty thousand drug abusers commit suicide each year. Close to eight hundred teenagers have unwanted pregnancies; most due to inadequate sexual knowledge. Child molestation is much too prevalent, and it is estimated that fifty percent of marriages end in divorce. These and other events might be better handled if children were better informed, and have knowledge of what to do if similar situations present themselves in the future. The benefits of such a program of instructing children in proper life styles would save the government billions of dollars, and make for a more stable and knowledgeable society.

Ideally, parents should be responsible for passing vital information of life's mastering skills down to their children. Unfortunately, many parents, either because of time restraints, feelings of insecurity, religious beliefs, unfamiliarity with particular subjects, or embarrassment, do not give their children all the necessary mastering skills needed to navigate life's paths. For example, very few parents instruct their off-springs in sexual behavior, sexual diseases, pregnancy prevention or sexual molestation.

In fact, many parents, purposely, refuse to expose their children to possible future dangers. The parental reasons to shelter children from possible future harm are multiple. Some use religious beliefs. Another group fears exposing children to an aberrant way of life might encourage them to pursue that life style.

Many children today are mentally distressed because they were sexually molested by an adult, who might have been a close relative, a religious leader or a friend of the family. If children were prepared vicariously how to handle aberrant sexual situations, prior to the event, they might have refused to engage in the act, and inform their parents about the episode.

If sexually abused children are identified, proper therapy might relieve them of future feelings of guilt and shame, that untreated children have been known to suffer with for the rest of their lives.

Children must be encouraged not to be embarrassed or feel guilty to discuss abnormal behavior or other uncomfortable encounters initiated by a friend, a relative, or stranger.

Unfortunately, too many family units are dysfunctional and, occasionally, children may be exposed to a drunken parent, or parental abuse. These children are good candidates for schooling instruction in mastering life's skills, as it is doubtful that they will ever receive adequate training at home. Significantly, the children from "toxic" homes have the highest percentage of delinquency when they are older, and would benefit greatly from participating in a Social and Emotional Learning (SEL) Program.

SOCIAL & EMOTIONAL LEARNING

(SEL PROGRAM)

Teachers should be trained to conduct classes

in Social and Emotional Learning Programs (mastering life's skills), which should be an integral part of the school curriculum. The program need only require less than one hour a month, during the school year, beginning in the first grade and concluding in the senior year. During the high school years, students may choose to take an elective course in life management skills and delve into subjects more intensely.

All students would be encouraged to participate in class discussions, and the topics may be suggested by an educator or the students themselves. A curriculum of proposed topics for the school year. would be drawn up by each school district, with input from the parents.

A class session in teaching life mastering skills might be conducted as follows. A teacher reads a paragraph, page, or chapter of a topic from a teacher's manual or from any other source, such as a newspaper, magazine, or internet posting, which adheres to the curriculum. The topic is then discussed mainly by the students; the educator need not participate unless additional facts are needed, or the desired outcomes are not being achieved. Each student will be encouraged to participate in the discussion, during the class period. The educator will learn much about the personality of each student. A shy child might be encouraged to participate more in group sessions. An aggressive child can be instructed in how to handle life skills in a more conciliatory manner, and so forth. A disturbed children could be referred for therapy.

Students would be asked to focus their suggestions, answering the five W's, "who, when, why, where, and what", concerning a subject.

For example, on the topic of substance abuse, students are asked to discuss: (1) **who** is likely to become addicted and name substances that can cause addiction?, (2)**what** is drug abuse and what should one do if approached to use the substance ?; (3) **why** would anyone want to use addicting substances ?, (4) **where** does one find help to treat the addiction? (5) **when** should professional help be needed?

The session should be light in tone and in good humor, and yet, be informative and instructive. Depending on the age of students, the teacher can conclude the class discussion, by asking the younger students to do a project, such as drawing a picture related to the subject presented , or in the older classes, a written assignment.

Forty-minutes a month, during the school year, should be adequate time to present the program and, vicariously, instill in the children the lessons to be learned. Important topics can be discussed as many times as a school curricula proposes, or as often as an educator feels is warranted.

By presenting a particular situation and having students thoroughly discuss all alternate solutions, whether they be undesirable or desirable, the child will be exposed to a set of facts, be made aware of what options are available, and proceed in a correct direction to handle the event. Thus, the student will know what to do if a similar situation arises, in the future.

The Board of Education, the Parents-Teacher's Association and the School Superintendents will determine the curriculum of the Social and Emotional Learning Programs, within their school district. If a subject is too emotionally charged, such as Sex Education, the subject does not have to be included within the Program. However, those parents that are willing to instruct their own children at home, can be given advise, at a special PTA meeting, on how to conduct particular learning sessions .

What has teaching Mastering Life Skills to children do with healing Federal ailments? What so important about the "Social and Emotional Learning Program" (as known as, Life Mastering Skills)?

The program is an answer to healing many of the problems that America faces today. By instructing children in skills to prevent possible future calamities, the American population will be more knowledgeable in the workings of the government, know how to identify truth from fiction, be more aware of the qualities of the people they elect to govern, when they are older and have the right to vote. This future group will be a far more stabilizing force in American society. Children as well as adults will be armed with the knowledge of how to avoid harmful situations, know how to achieve good relationships with friends and significant others, and understand the importance of our form of government and ways to preserve and improve it.

Monetarily, the United States government spends billions of dollars in fighting drug abuse, prejudice, gun violence, and other social issues. Much of this money would not be needed if such a program of teaching social skills to our children were universally adopted throughout the country.

The United States Government will probably

change over the course of time; hopefully for the better. Americans have to be careful not to lose freedoms, that we presently enjoy. Unfortunately, forces of totalitarianism and other dictatorial forms of government are constant potential threats, and the best forms of treatment to prevent the loss of democracy is to have a well educated and knowledgeable populace; a most powerful reason to institute a course in social skills.

It is important to understand that group discussions of life mastering skills are not "brain washing", as many opponents would falsely suggest. The children, themselves, analyze a situation, become familiar with the subject and formulate their own conclusions.

Chapter 3

FUNDING ELECTIONS

The Constitution of the United States of America is a remarkable document and has served its citizens well for the past 247 years. The outstanding feature that makes the Constitution durable, is its ability to be adapted to modern needs.

The Country, for the most part, has a two party system which formulates the policies of America. Minor parties have occasionally been on the ballot. Rarely has a new political party been able to obtain control of power.

In the mid nineteenth century, a coalition of disillusioned Americans who opposed and disliked President Andrew Jackson (1767 to 1845) formed in 1834 the Whig party. The group was a coalition of numerous interests. Protestant moral reformers demanded that laws be passed to prohibit Catholic immigration. Others were incensed about Jackson's Trail of Tears, in which Native Americans were forced on a death march.

Abolition of slavery was not a prominent policy of the Whigs, as some of its members favored slavery. Both southerners and northerners made up its constituents.

In 1840 the Whigs were able to elect its first president, William Henry Harrison, who died of pneumonia in office after thirty days. John Tyler was the first vice president to become chief executive, as a result of a presidential death. He also has the distinction of being the first sitting President to be married while in the oval office.

In 1854, opposed to expansion of slavery within the States, the Republican party was founded.   But unlike the present day Republicans, the original party advocated strong federal intervention, and supported federal funded higher education, national transportation,   and   increased   income taxation. The Civil War was fought to keep the Union together, but resulted in freeing the slaves in all the States, when Lincoln enacted the Emancipation Proclamation in 1863. Today's Republican Party in no way resembles the party of Abraham Lincoln. In 2022, Republicans, strongly supports state's rights, protection of white supremacists, limitation of universal voting and policies that attract staunch religious groups.

Today, America has been torn apart by extreme right and left factions. Both sides are determined to impose their demands upon all citizens, and make their policies the law of the land. Recently, a Senate Majority Leader, openly defied the policies of the opposite party, even though, he supported these same exact policies in the past. This same party strongly refuses to pass gun restriction laws, in the face of mass shootings in schools and elsewhere, while accepting donations from the National Rifle Association.

The United States Senate was designed to be an organization of decor; treating all its members with civility. Unfortunately, this is no longer the case. Some members of this austere governmental body now exhibit rudeness and hostility, foster lies, and unfortunately, openly or tacitly supported the insurrection of the Capital of January 6, 2001. They do not honor their pledge of allegiance to America; a solemn pledge which they swore when they took office.

This is not surprising as America has always

been a country of conflict, a country with divergent opinions and attitudes. But this very aspect is what makes this Country great. Usually, in times of need, Americans overcome their diversity and come together.

In the late 1930's, when Hitler was conquering the nations of Europe and slaughtering Jews, America was torn as to what should be done.   Many Americans turned their backs and wanted no part of a conflict that was an ocean away. Prominent individuals, such as the famed aviator, Charles A. Lindbergh supported the Nazi cause. The American icon, Henry Ford , a devout anti-Semite, and a fan of Adolf Hitler, favored the Nazis.   Adolf Hitler complimented Ford by name in his infamous book, <u>Mein Kampf.</u>

Others recognized the danger of the Nazi war machine, and felt that America should make a   stance in favor of democracy, and the elimination of a ruthless dictator. The United States Congress wanted no part of the conflict. Fortunately, the forces of decency and foresight won out. America and it's allies defeated Hitler's dictatorial regime and, for the past seventy years, America and the free world saw an expansion of democracy throughout the globe.

Before the seventeenth century, no government existed where the majority of citizens were given the power to choose their leaders. In America, the power of the vote, at the origin of the country, was denied to women, African Americans and other disenfranchised groups. However, with alteration of the original Constitution, many of the previous wrongs have been eliminated.

Unfortunately, at the present time in some countries, the pendulum appears to be turning away from democracy toward autocracy.

Politics has become a big business, and money has become a major player in all elections, especially with members of Congress and local governmental officials. It is estimated that to elect a Senator in 2018, the campaign costs fifteen million dollars. Running for the House of Representative was far cheaper, only two million dollars. A Republican Senator of Florida holds the winning record for spending on a campaign, a mere 83.5 million. One governor, at the present time this chapter is being written, has over 100 million dollars at his disposal to use in a future election. The salary of an average United States Senator and Representative is 174,000 dollars. From a business point of view, it makes no sense to spend millions of dollars to be remunerated a nominal salary, unless you are spending other people's money and benefiting financially.

People who try to influence elected governmental officials are called lobbyists. In 2021, the National Rifle Association spent 3.31 million U.S. dollars lobbying Congress not to approve gun safety legislation.

And so, lets address one on the major problems of our political system. And let's call it by its true name...bribery, or in legalese, "Quid Pro Quo", one favor in turn for another.

As a result, one major ailment of the United States Government is the corruption of many of our legal representatives by those who donate money to politicians. Unfortunately, many elected individuals, who rightly should represent the constituents that voted for them, favor their big donors.

Chapter 4

POLITICAL CAMPAIGNING

Far too much money is being spent to elect a member of Congress. The donation puts pressure on an elected person to do the bidding of the organization giving the money. The NRA (National Rifle Association) spent millions of dollars, lobbying Congress not to support gun legislation, even those measures that make common sense, such as backgrounds checks and banning military assault weapons. One congressman received 1.2 million to fund his campaign. This Congressional individual voted not to protect children in schools against senseless gun killings. It is estimated that over an eighteen year period, the NRA contributed 13 million dollars to Congressional campaigns, which does not include the amount spent on lobbying and other perks.

Congress has the power to enact campaign finance laws and the Federal Election Commission has the power to enforce the election laws passed by Congress. Most campaign funds are financed through donors. Only the office of the Presidency can qualify for federal funds, if qualified, both for the primaries and the general election.

Federal laws do not permit corporations or labor unions to give money directly to candidates running for Federal offices. The amount of money donated by individuals and political action organizations are likewise limited. However, some groups are allowed to give money to support a politician. A donor may be an individual, a candidate committee, a national party committee or a Political Action Committee (PAC) and Super PAC.

PAC are tax-exempt political committees whose purpose is to raise money to benefit a political candidate. A Super PAC is a political organization that may raise unlimited sums of money from labor unions,corporations, and individuals. The only restriction is that the organization cannot contribute directly to a candidate or party. In 2020, super PACs spent more than $2 billion.

Recently, a Canadian steel industry billionaire steered $1.75 million to a candidate's campaign, in violation of Congressional funding laws. The foreigner gave donations from   his Pennsylvania-based subsidiary to influence a Presidential candidate to curb import of foreign steel, which would help his sales, and to change highway safety rules, which was giving truckers a hard time moving tubular steel. The FEC imposed a fine close to $975,000   because of the foreign nation status.

The amount of monies available to a political candidate is known as "a war chest", and the more money a candidate can use in a campaign, for newspaper, television, radio, internet, handout fliers, fund raising events, and so forth, the better the odds that the candidate will be successful in a political race. In other words, money plays a very important part in electing a candidate.

Unfortunately, a few politicians do not legally abide   by the   the election laws, knowing full well that they will get away with the deed. A State Governor used funds from Federal coffers to pay for a State election, which is not legal. No one challenged it.

Since personal contributions are limited   in the amount that can be donate, someone came up with the gimmick of bundling, in which groups of people can donate funds to an organization, which in turn, gives the money to a candidate. Lobbyists also get into the act by arranging fundraising events, assembling PAC's and encouraging people to donate.

ACUTE PRESCRIPTION
POLITICAL FUNDING

What can acutely be done to stop the unfair donation of monies to candidates who, supposedly, are elected to serve the people they represent, and not those that buy Congressional votes?

One possible solution follows. Any representative who receives more than one thousand dollars in campaign contributions from an individual or organization, should voluntarily be excused from voting on a bill which would benefit that individual or organization. Lobbyists can continue interviewing members of Congress, but, by law, should not be allowed to donate more than $1000 to a political campaign. If elected officials receive more than the allotted sum from any one group, the individuals must recuse themselves from voting on the issue, for which the donor is asking a favor.

The Office of Management and Budget should require all Congressional members to submit a list of all donors and the amount of donations given. Excessive amounts will be given to the department in charge of paying for campaign finances, to be, if needed, distributed equally among the candidates.

In 1949, communication outlets, such as radio and television, had to present unbiased contrasting views of political contests, referred to as the "fairness doctrine". The policy was abolished in 2011, and indeed, is one of the factors that has led our nation to the present day state of polarization. This ruling of equal representation should be reinstated in all media outlets. This is known as the   "equal-time rule." If one party candidate or a supporting group is allowed to broadcast the views of a candidate, then an opponent can request equal time to present opposing views.

Lying has become a prominent feature in political   communication   outlets.   These broadcasting systems must be held accountable for spreading lies, and purposely making damaging remarks that are untrue. The communication media outlet must acknowledge a falsehood of a guest speaker immediately, inform their audiences of the lie every day for a week, and not allow that guest to entertain their audiences for a period of time, as determined by Congress.

CHRONIC PRESCRIPTION POLITICAL FUNDING

The acute prescription to political funding handles the immediate actions that need to be taken. Chronic prescriptions are long term goals.

Campaigning should be restricted to two to three months before a vote is scheduled. At the present time, electioneering starts far too early, sometimes, years in advance. The government should be responsible for the payment of all campaign costs, which would include mailings and advertising on television, radio and internet, Each candidate could have a private war chest of no more than 50,000 dollars. This money must come from donations by constituents, living within the district of the candidate. Funds donated outside the congressional person's district, will be confiscated by the committee that is responsible for funding elections. All donations will be transparent and published at the expense of the government.

Wealthy donors who previously gave huge amount of funds to politicians, can now donate the funds to the Federal Election Commission, who will oversee the fair distribution of political campaigns. The top three political parties, as determined by voter primaries, would be eligible to receive governmental funds.

The playing field for all candidates must be equal. Everyone can only spend no more than $100,000 donated by their district supporters plus $50,000 supplemented by the Federal government. Any non-district individual or corporation wishing to give money toward a campaign, can contribute to the government agency in charge of campaign funds. If additional funds are needed for campaigning, Congress will appropriate the necessary amounts of money, equally to all candidates, assuming that the reason for the added cash is legitimately needed

If politically negative or false ads are inserted into a campaign, they will be immediately withdrawn, and the perpetrator will be fined. American children must be exposed to the workings of the Federal government, both in civic courses, as well as sessions given in a Social and Emotional Learning Program. Teaching fundamental principles of government are important and, hopefully, will instill patriotic feelings for the country, and restore faith in the American political process.

Chapter 5

TERM LIMITS

America should be a country that is controlled by its citizens. "A Country of the people, by the people and for the people"; a quote by Abraham Lincoln's, given in his Gettysburg Address. The original phrase was given in a sermon on Independence Day, July 4, 1858 by Minister Theodore Parker. Lincoln in his speech of 1863 also charged that "under God", American democracy "shall not perish from the earth." Lets hope that these prophetic words are applicable forever.

Ancient Athens and Sparta rotated the entire membership of their governing councils every year. Ancient Rome favored to elect its governing officials for a one year period, and these individuals could not hold a governmental position for ten years. Most historians feel that the term limits were adopted to prevent corruption.

In Colonial Times, most legislatures were familiar with the history of antiquity. In the Colony of Connecticut, the governor could hold his office for a period of one year. In Pennsylvania, shortly after independence from England was declared, the governing body limited a term for its members in the general assembly at four years, and prevented the re-election of the same individual for seven years.

The Articles of Confederation of 1781 limited congressional terms to no more than three years every six years. The Constitution adopted in 1789 omitted term limits. Most historians believe that George Washington set a precedent of a two term limit for the Presidency. The truth be told, he was just too tired and worn out, when he declined a third term. In 1951, the Twenty-Second Amendment established a two term limit of the President of the United States. This was prompted by the four terms served by Franklin D. Roosevelt (1933 to 1945).

The concept of term limits is slowly becoming more popular with the electorate. However, Congress has failed to enact term limitations and the Supreme Court of the United States, on a 5-4 vote, ruled that states governments could not set term limits on members of the federal government.

At the present time, only the President is limited to two four year terms. The Vice-President can service unlimited four year terms, the House of Representatives, unlimited two year terms, and the Senate, unlimited six year terms. The Supreme Court and Federal judicial appointments, retain the office until they retire or die.

The longest period of time served by a senator was fifty one years, nine have held a Senatorial seat for over forty years, and fifteen others over thirty years.

ACUTE PRESCRIPTION
TERM LIMITS

I doubt if anything to correct term limits will be done at the present time. I cannot conceive of anyone wanting to end chances of being re-elected. Who would, in their right mind, would want to give up a great job with all its perks, its powers, and financial gains? Politicians scream when someone talks about socialism, but our central governmental bodies enjoy quasi-socialized medicine (75% subsidized health insurance), great salaries, pension   plan   benefits,   workman's compensations if hurt while in office, free travel for themselves and staffers, special license plates that allow the Congressional members to park their car free, in illegal areas, a $25 per month gym and swimming membership, and many more free advantageous. Congress also has passed laws to protect themselves from Freedom of Information Act, some forms of subpoenas, and protection against whistle blowers. These are just a few of the many benefits that our representatives enjoy.

One congressional person with bipolar disorder and depression was awarded a big award because the individual "argued that the dealings of Congress made him ill".

CHRONIC PRESCRIPTION
TERM LIMITS

The populace must be made aware of the dangers of having their Representatives in power for a long time. Legislatures who campaign on passing bills which limit the length of political terms should be favored to be voted in, and if they do not abide by their promise, should be not be approved at the next political race, in which they are running.

If a Representative or Senator is retiring, he may be more likely to vote for term limits.

The U.S. Constitution does not limit the number of terms a United States Senator or Representative can serve. Therefore, an Amendment to the Constitution is not needed. A majority vote in the House of Representatives and the Senate has the ability to limit the number of years of a Federal elected office.

The following suggestions should be considered. Representative, Senators and all Federal Judges serve no longer than twelve years in any Federal elected position. Senators are voted in every six years and, under term limits, would only be able to serve for two terms. House Representatives are voted from their district every two years and can hold six consecutive terms, if they are re-elected. The total allotted time to be allowed to hold office in Congress would be twelve years. For example, if a Representative held office for eight years, he would be disqualified to hold an additional Senate seat, assuming the individual was elected to the position, as the term limit rule ends in four years, and a Senator must serve for six years.

Federal Judges, including those of the Supreme Court, would also be required to serve only for twelve years, and then must retire from the Bench.

Once the term of twelve years for any Federal elected official is completed, the candidates must have no further Federal Governmental involvement for the next six years, after which they may serve another twelve years if elected, appointed or confirmed.

In addition, no retired Federal office holder may join a registered lobbying organization for three years after they retire from their elected or appointed governmental position. The purpose is to prevent any possible impropriety on the part of the retiring individual.

Chapter 6

MONEY, MONEY, MONEY

Prior to the Revolutionary War of 1775, English, French and Spanish monies were the main forms of currency used in the American colonies. Following the break with England, the Continental Congress issued "Continental Currency", which was printed on printing plates, actually designed by Paul Revere. In 1792, Congress adopted the dollar note and coins, based on the English (imperial) system, as the primary units of currency. Today, most other countries use the metric system, which was adopted in France in 1799.

Paper money was first issued by the Federal government in 1861. Before that time, private banks printed their own bills of paper currency. At one time there were 7000 different bank notes in circulation, within the United States, each with their own design.

The initial stimulus for the Federal Government to print its own money was the need to finance the Civil War. Paper bills replaced the heavy weighted coins. For the next sixty five years, banks were again allowed to print their own monies; however, at the present time, all private banks have to use Federal generated money. The Federal Reserve Bank began issuing notes in 1914, and today is the only permissible printed currency in circulation within the United States.

For the first one hundred and fifty years, America was on the gold standard, which meant that the government would convert a paper bill into a fixed amount of gold, on demand. In 1933, The United States, struggling with the Great Depression, eliminated the gold standard and began printing paper money, that is accepted only on faith. In 1971, during the Nixon Presidency, congress passed a law that no longer allowed the U.S. Dollar to be converted into gold.

Each country tends to have its own currencies, in the form of paper and metal coins, that it mints. The dollar bills issued by the United States Government is presently "the gold standard", but all countries use a changeable exchange rate between the different currencies. In Europe in 1999, eleven countries, not including Denmark and United Kingdom, joined together and issued one paper currency, the Euro, and standardized coins in 2002. Subsequently, Slovenia, Malta, Cyprus, Slovakia, Estonia, Latvia and Lithuania, joined the European Union and replaced their old currency with the Euro.

The exchange rate between countries is determined by many factors, and changes in value, depending on the economic actions of a government or central bank. Currencies no longer have to be backed by gold or other precious metals, but could be backed by other currencies such as the United States dollar or the United Kingdom pound.

CREDIT CARDS

Credit cards were first introduced in the 1920's when companies introduced private company cards, but the first modern credit card, which could be used at multiple retailers, was distributed in 1950. By 2017, each American had, on average, three credit cards and the total credit card debt in America reached one trillion dollars. The average interest rate on moneys owed to the credit card companies range from 14 to 24 percent. If the credit card is paid in full within the month due, there is no interest charge.

DIGITAL CURRENCIES

With the invention of the computer, digital currencies came onto the scene. Unlike paper or coin currencies, digital money has no physical form. The electronic transfer of funds moves quickly over the internet, and can be used to buy goods and services. The United States Federal Government, as of yet, is not involved in digital currencies.

The idea of digital money came to fruition in the early 1980's. The first electronic cash company was founded in 1989, but declared bankruptcy ten years later.

Bitcoin entered the scene in 2009, and its claim to fame was the absence of a central server and no tangible assets. Because of a lack of central control, governmental regulation has proven to be difficult.

Other electronic currencies have been started. Some have been accused of being a Ponzi and a money laundering scheme, and prosecuted by some governments. A Ponzi scheme is fraudulent activity in which investors think that legitimate profits are being made, but in actuality, the monies earned are coming from new investors. The term "Ponzi" draws its name from Charles Ponzi, who in the prior Depression era of the 1920"s promised a fifty percent profit on an investment within 45 days, and one hundred percent return in 90 days. He was paying original investors with new monies collected from new investors, not profits. Ponzi was eventually convicted of mail fraud charges. Charles Ponzi was not the first one to conduct this type of scheme, and, as history proves, will not be the last.

As of yet, digital currencies are not widely used. Some investors are concerned with the extreme volatility, instability, and lack of centralization. Bitcoin has better trust worthiness because of security measures. However, the energy consumed by Bitcoin transactions requires vast amount of electrical energy. One study estimates that the amount of electrical energy used in Bitcoin transactions is equivalent to the amount of energy consumed by a small country.

Using bitcoins is referred to as "mining." The electronic transfer can be used to buy goods and services, and be exchanged for other currencies. The Republic of El Salvador, in Central America, adopted bitcoin as a legal form of currency in June 2021.

In early 2022, a bitcoin was worth close to 40,000 dollars. A few months later, the value dropped to 19,000. The sudden volatility of this electronic form of currency has brought El Salvador close to bankruptcy.

The total bitcoin supply is fixed to twenty one million units. No additional electronic bitcoins will be "mined". Because of the limited number, the cryptocurrency has experienced crashes and rallies. In 2011, a bitcoin was worth twenty nine dollars. Five months later, the price fell to $2.05. One year later, the "coin" was worth $13.50, but over several months was selling for $1200, and then fell to $700 three days later. In December 2021, a bitcoin was worth $50,000. Day traders have used the volatile fluctuations to make profit, just as they do in the stock and commodity markets.

ACUTE PRESCRIPTION
MONEY, MONEY

America is one of the richest country in the world. Over 30% of households have yearly incomes exceeding $100,000. However, the bottom fifty percent of the population share only 2% of the wealth, while the top 1% of individuals controls 35%.

Unfortunately, greed is a dominate force in America and the "haves" , like many societies before them, refuse to share reasonably with the "have-nots". The wealthy claim that the poor are lazy and just want government handouts. They show little compassion for the majority who, even with more than one job, can hardly feed their families.

As of today, in America, more than 38 million people, including 12 million children are food deprived. Many Americans do not have the money to buy the necessary food, and must choose between buying food, paying rent, seeing a doctor, or purchasing medications.

When wages are raised, the individuals

making the most usually get a larger wage increase, percentage-wise, than those at the bottom of the wage scale. Many times, inflation is the stimulus for the raise , which negates any benefits to the lower class.

Certain occupations are overpaid and many are underpaid.   Income tends to be proportionate to the amount of education of an individual. Therefore, college graduates tend to be the highest paid. Men, statistically, are paid more than women for the same duties and responsibilities. This inequality is slowly disappearing, but not fast enough.

The top 1% of Americans, approximately 1.4 million households, earn over $500,000 a year; the average income of this group is $1.7 million. Corporations are giving their CEO's unbelievable salaries. The ten highest paid executives had yearly compensation of over $100 million in 2021; the average being $330 million.

The majority of our elected Senators and Representatives in Congress are millionaires and, proportionately, their medium wealth increases every year, as the medium assets of the people they represent keeps falling.

The acute solution is for a change in the tax code of Federal Government. However, as long as our Representatives and Senators rely on the wealthy to support their political campaigns and continues to enjoy benefits not available to average citizens, needed changes in the law will doubtfully take place.

Congress has in the past refused to adequately fund the Internal Revenue Service (IRS), and, at times, has even forced the agency to decrease the number of employees. The less agents employed by the Internal Revenue Service, the less tax forms can be examined. The less tax forms examined, the less number of wealthy individuals can be audited and the less money due can be collected.   Over the next ten years, the government accounting office estimates that 80 billion dollars invested in the IRS would yield 200 billion in funds not previously collected.

CHRONIC PRESCRIPTION
MONEY, MONEY

United States citizens should be grateful that they live in the greatest country in the world.

But, they also need to remember that a stable government requires a more equitable distribution of wealth, so that no one should be deprived of the basic needs of living, such as food, housing, clothing, proper education, and medical care.

Taxing those that produce excessive wealth and distributing it to those who are in poverty is not only morally correct, but is a sign of greatness of a righteous nation.

Money, whether it be paper, coin, or non-tangible assets, such as electronic bits, all have the same purpose. Money is a vehicle used to purchase a physical item or concept, and its value is worth whatever individuals deem. No longer being on the gold standard, the actual value of any form of currency assumes that others will also agree to accepting its value.

All moneys will change in value, depending on economic events. Governments no longer have to back their currency with a tangible asset, such as gold or silver, but can print money as its needs, resulting in fiscal devaluation. All moneys will change in value, depending on the status of the economy of a country.

Digital currencies, or cryptocurrencies, have come onto the monetary scene, and, as of yet, does not have a long stable tract record. What use is cryptocurrency? Investors use it to hedge against inflation, store value, and to circumvent traditional banking.   Electronic money has also been popular   in illegal enterprises, such as money "laundering", since, at the present time, it is impossible to tract the path of cryptocurrencies.

As of now, cryptocurrency is hard to trace, and the "miners" are asked to report gains and losses on Federal Income Tax forms. Until electronic monies can officially be monitored, the IRS must rely on the honesty of the individual reporting electronic transactions. The IRS uses agents to spot check individual returns. If a purchaser of cryptocurrencies is found to have misrepresented the true gain of a transaction, stiff fines are imposed.

CHAPTER 7

FEDERAL TAXES

Many citizens complain about paying federal income tax, but, surveys show that most appear to be honest, especially, on their tax forms. They are more likely to cheat on diets, tests and surveys. However, many tax laws are vaguely written, and shrewd tax preparers take advantage of the ambiguity.

However, because of ill-defined tax laws and the many loop holes that congress enacts, the rates usually favors the most wealthy. The top earners pay less percentage of taxes, than the people who work for them. Billionaires pay on average an 8.2 percent tax rate. Most of their income is not taxed, since investments do not yield taxes until they are sold, and, usually, if a profit is realized, the investment is not sold. This chapter focuses on personal income tax and dose not concern itself with corporate income tax or other forms of levies.

The United States has a progressive tax system. There are seven tax rate brackets, ranging from 10 % to 37%. Half of the top tax payers paid more than 97% of the taxes collected. The average worker paid 28% of his wages to the United States Treasury. At the present time, a family making less than $10,000 a year pays a tax rate of ten percent, 24% if the family income ranges between $86,000 and $165,000, 35% for an income of $209,000 to $524,000, and 37% if the income is above $524,000 or more.

The United States has lower tax rates than many countries and ranks number 32 on a list of 41 countries of the world. Last year, countries that had higher income tax rates than America were Australia, and Norway; countries with lower tax rates included Canada and Syria.

The Federal Government, also, has a lower tax rate on goods and services than most other nations. The United States collects 18% of its revenues from this form of taxation. Most countries have a value-added tax (VAT), which the United States does not have. A value-added tax is levied at each stage of production, distribution and sales. All of which is paid by the consumer. It is comparable to a sales tax.

The United States has one of the most complicated tax-filing systems in the world. The Constitution gave Congress the power to collect taxes. After the Civil war, the first income tax was instituted and the Office of Internal Revenue Service was established. The office collects taxes from citizens and, when first imposed, consisted mainly of taxes on commodities, such as tobacco, alcohol, tea, and gunpowder. Taxation on individual's income was made law in 1913.

The estate tax was first enacted in 1797 to fund the U.S. Navy. Over the years, numerous other taxes have came into existence; the sales tax in 1921, the gift tax in 1924, and the social security tax in 1937. In 1913 Federal Income Tax was imposed to pay for WWI. Taxes on alcohol, tobacco, gasoline, and telephone, are presently combined within the price, so that many people did not even realize that they are paying taxes on these items.

Calculation needed for a tax return has become very complicated; so much so, that individuals turn to the use of Certified Public Accountants or electronic tax programs, like Turbo Tax and H&R Block, to comply with the numerous tax filing regulations.

ACUTE PRESCRIPTION
FEDERAL TAXES

Congress should realize that the health of the country and its citizens depends on sensible income tax laws, that can provide the necessary funds to continue to make the United States a strong, powerful, and yet compassionate country. Everyone should be willing to pay taxes that they are mandated to pay so that America can continue to be a world leader and a champion of democracy.

In the short run, Congress should fund the Internal Revenue Service with the needed budget to expand its work force, in order that more tax returns can be examined. The tax codes are so complex and intricate that errors are bound to be innocently made, or perhaps, not so innocently. With added tax examiners working for the IRS, far more income tax forms can be scrutinized.

Beneath $500,000   in total income, tax returns can be randomly examined. The majority of returns can be scanned by computer, and if the figures submitted by the tax payer does not match the information submitted from income producing sources, then a personal audit would be indicated. All income tax forms with a total income above 500,000 dollars should automatically be examined by an Internal Revenue Service agent.

CHRONIC PRESCRIPTION
FEDERAL TAXES

To reiterate, America has one of the most complex system of collecting taxes than any other country in the world, but has the distinction of having the one of the lowest tax revenue to gross domestic product (GDP) ratio of any of the democratic countries.

In America, taxes are paid on federal, state and local community levels. Taxes are based on salary, sales of items purchased, dividends from investments, imports, estates, and gifts, as well as, property values.

The Federal and State tax codes are so

complex that most people need professional help to be able to fill out the forms correctly. The average person, who does not own a business, has to devote approximately fifteen hours to complete the IRS tax forms. Even if one uses a professional tax accountant, the individual must still spend much time gathering all the necessary data required.

Congress should revamp the tax code, so that the average American should be able to complete a tax form quickly and correctly. Individuals or joint filers who have nothing to report except earnings listed on the IRS W-4 tax form (employee's withholding) and/or interests and dividends, should be able to fill out a simple post card or electronic form, and quickly receive a refund promptly.

America is notorious for its tax loop holes, that is a tax laws that allows a group to avoid paying their true tax liability. These loopholes are legal and is a popular method for individuals or corporations to avoid paying the actual taxes, that would be normally due. For example, many American companies moved offices and factories overseas in order to avoid paying taxes. The corporation improves its bottom financial line and pays less taxes, but jobs and tax revenues in America are lost.

Many times, the fault of tax evasion lie in the wording of the tax legislation. The loophole was not purposely intended , but may not have been   foreseen at the drafting of the law.

The richest multi-billionaires in America, proportionately, paid no or very little Federal income taxes, while the median American household with a yearly income of 60 to 70,000 dollars, paid 14 % in Federal taxes.

From 2014 to 2018, the very rich had an increase in their wealth by 400 billion dollars, but paid only 4% in taxes. In contrast, a comparable number of low wage earners, during the same time period, saw their net worth rise $65,000 dollars, mainly due to an increase in the value of their homes. Because of increased wage earnings, their average tax bill for the same five year period increased just over $62,000, negating any increase in total wealth. The reason for the disparity comes from the fact that one only pays taxes on an asset when it is sold. Loopholes in the tax system must be carefully examined and eliminated when unfair.

Whether an individual is wealthy or poor every individual should pay their fare share of taxes, the wealthier paying a greater percentage that those in the lower tax brackets.

Tax returns should include not only what an individual or corporation earns, but should also include the net-worth, with a complete listing of holdings. Assets sent overseas would be taxed as income gained, and when sold would be subject to the tax statues concerning gain and loss rules.

Congress should set tax rates that are fair and reasonable. Higher rates should be applied to wealthier individuals and lower rates to individuals that have lesser incomes.

(percentage of taxes for different wage earners. The rates listed in the chart on the following page are suggestions for the purpose of demonstration and should not be considered the actual rates that Congress should enact.)

Chart 1. Wages and Tax Amount, graduated.
(for demonstration purposes only)

Wages (dollars)	Tax %
Under 30,000	2
30,001 to 99,999	15
100,000 to 199,999	25
200,000 to 599,999	35
600,000 to 799,999	40
800,000 to 999,999	45
1,000,000 to 4,999,999	55
5,000,000 to 19,999,999	65
20,000,000 plus	70

(explanation of chart - if the take home salary is 70,000, the income tax would be 15% of 70,000. If take home pay is 350,000, tax would be 35% of 350,000)

Taxation would be graduated, and by law, will be set by Congress. Every citizen would be required to pay income tax and the amount of income tax levied would increases as an individual or joint tax-payers have increased revenue.

Even though taxes are not paid until an asset is sold, all individuals and corporations must pay a minimal percentage of income gained, even if they did not sell the asset. When the asset is actually sold, that amount originally paid would be deducted from the actual amount on selling, whether it be a gain or loss. This guarantees that the wealthy pay some tax and do not get away with paying no tax.

Yearly increase in asset wealth	Tax %
Under 99,999	0
1,000,000 to 4,999,999	25
5,000,000 to 19,999,999	30
20,000,000 plus	40

(explanation of chart - if net worth increases in the previous year by 1,500,000, then the minimum tax must be 25% of 1,500.000).

Tax avoidance loopholes must be closed. Many tax avoidance gimmicks have been adapted by the wealthy. Millions of dollars are charged by accountants to set up trusts to work around the tax requirements. Family trusts and other types of trusts have been established, which, some times, are no more than subterfuges to avert income tax. For example, family members, of college age, get tuition grants by submitting an essay to a family trust, which supposedly is open to individuals that qualify, but the winner of the contest just happens to be a relative of the trustor. The family members win. The trustor gets a tax deduction from the monies put into the trust. The trust pays for the child's schooling, which, in essence is, tax-free money.

The top one percent of income earners in America like to brag that their secretaries are paying more income tax percentage-wise than themselves. The Congress has the obligation to correct this inequity.

But don 't hold your breath for changes to be made. Congress tends to favor the wealthy, who contribute to election campaigns. In addition, congressional members, for the most part, fall into higher income tax brackets, and would be hesitant to raise their own taxes.

Some of the wealthy claim that the lower classes are "lazy" and don't deserve federal assistance. Others are incensed that they have to pay taxes for expenses of the government.

In a New England state, at a recent town meeting, the local powers-to-be, with the support of the town's people, fired their only police officer, slashed the school budget, and removed extra curricular activities from the school curricular, such as intramural sports, tennis, math and tract teams, and creative writing. The group's rational was that these activities cost money and these subjects "were not necessary to participate in a free government".

As it turns out, the leader of this movement, as a child, attended a government supported school, joined the school tennis team, played intramural sports, and engaged in many other extracurricular activities. All of which was paid for by taxes collected from the community. In addition, many people, who have "no children, see no reason to support higher taxes to benefit other people's children".

A lot of attention has been paid to "Russian oligarchs". An oligarch is defined as a very rich business leader with a great deal of political influence. But, America has its own oligarchs, and many of them.

In 2018, the highest paid CEO of a company receive a salary of 513 million dollars. His "comrades" in this same class received approximately 140 to 260 million dollars a year. The medium take home pay of a chief executive officer (CEO) of all the major corporations were given 60 to 93 million dollars a year. Women corporate leaders also received   hefty compensation, but far less than their male counterparts. These figures do not include stock options and other perks that come with the job. The medium American worker at an organization that its CEO receives over 500 million dollars a year is approximately 40,000 dollars a year. American oligarchs can easily contribute big dollars to support those politicians that will vote for the oligarch's political wishes.

CHAPTER 8

FEDERAL HOLIDAYS

The Federal Government has designated certain days as a Government Holiday, during which time Federal employees have a paid vacation day. State governments do not have to celebrate a Federal holiday.

The new year, at the present time, begins with the New Year Holiday on January first. But, this was not the always the case, as the new year, prior to the sixteenth century, began on April first. During that century, France switched from the Julian to the Gregorian Calendar. The Julian Calendar began in mid-March with the spring equinox, and was celebrated until the first of April; however, the two week April celebration of the Julian New Year interfered with the harvesting of crops. France and other countries, then, switched to the Gregorian Calendar, and celebrated The New Year on the first day of January.

News traveled slowly in the sixteenth century,

and many refused to believe the switch. They were eventually ridiculed and called "Fools of April", which is one theory of how April first became April's Fool Day; a day during which practical jokes were, and are stilled played on individuals.

There are twelve Federal holidays. In 1870, four holidays were enacted into law and, subsequently additional eight holidays were added. The holidays were celebrated in recognition of significant historical figures in American history or dates of historical importance. States do not have to partake in the events of the Federal holidays, and can celebrate other holidays of their choice. Alaska recognizes the last Monday in March as a remembrance to the purchase of Alaska from Russia.

Conditions of regulations of Federal holidays may vary from area to area. On Inauguration Day (January 20th every 4 years), only Federal workers in the Washington, D.C. area are exempt from work, so that they can attend the inauguration proceedings. A list of current Federal Holidays follows:

OFFICIAL FEDERAL HOLIDAYS

FEDERAL HOLIDAYS

calendar day	date celebrated	exceptions
New Year's Day -	January 1st	
Martin Luther King, Jr. Day	3rd Monday in January	
Inauguration Day -	January 20th.	Every four years
		Wash DC Fed Worker
Washington's Birthday	3rd Monday in February	
Memorial Day -	last Monday in May.	
Juneteenth -	June 18	June 19 on weekdays
Independence Day	July 4th	
Labor Day -	1st Monday in September	
Columbus Day	2nd Monday in October	
Veteran's Day -	Nov 11	
Thanksgiving's Day -	4th Thursday in November	
Christmas	December 25	Dec 24 on weekdays

(Congress determines Federal holidays. States do not have to observe the holiday; however, may celebrate the day if they choose.)

In 1938, November 11 became a holiday to

commemorate the end of the first World War (1917-1919) and to honor the soldiers that fought and died in that war.

Thanksgiving was first declared by George Washington in 1789 as a day of public prayers and offering of gratitude. However, it was acclaimed a national holiday by Presidential proclamation 76 years later. Abraham Lincoln declared that the last Thursday in November should be celebrated as a day of thanks and appreciation.

However, one additional important holiday should be added to the list of eleven Federal holidays. The Constitution mandates that Federal elections should be overseen by the States to protect voting rights.

In 1870, the 15th Amendment gave colored Americans the right to vote. However, many states imposed barriers, such as literacy tests and poll taxes, which make it harder for certain individuals to cast their choice of candidate.

In 1920, the 19th Amendment extended voting rights to women. The 24th Amendment eliminated the poll tax and, in 1971, the 26th Amendment lowered the voting age from twenty one to eighteen years of age.

Article I, section 4 of the Constitution empowers Congress and State Legislatures to regulate when and where elections should be held. In 1842, a law was passed to elect Representatives by districts. But the State Legislature has the power to draw the boundaries of these voting districts. The contrived district borders often favor the party in power, a process that has come to be known as Gerrymandering.

In 1812, a political cartoon in a local newspaper depicted a voting district that favored the election of the governor of Massachusetts, Bridgeable Gerry. The boundaries of district looked like a monster with a forked tongue. Since the cartoon resembled a Salamander, the editors labeled the formation of a voting district, "Gerrymandering".

The following chapter discusses the addition of a very important and necessary new holiday, that should be observed by both the Federal and State governments.

CHAPTER 9

FEDERAL VOTING

In the United States, the election day for the Federal Government was set for the Tuesday following the first Monday in November. Presidential elections are held every four years. US House of Representatives are voted into office every two years, while Senators have a six year term; one third voted in every two years.

Most states conduct voting on the same day as the Federal government. Special elections can be held anytime a Congressional seat becomes vacant.

Ten states states, the territory of Northern Mariana Islands and Puerto Rico celebrate election Tuesday as a public holiday. Other states, such as. California, make provisions for workers to take time off with pay to vote.

However, voting is such an important process in our democratic society, that it is time for voting day to become a national holiday.

Not only do I suggest that a National Federal Voting Holiday be declared, but those citizens that do not vote should be penalized, as they are shirking their civic responsibility. A penalty of twenty five dollars for the first occurrence for not participating in a vote should be imposed, and increasing amounts, thereafter, if voting avoidance persists.

Individuals unable to get to the polls must provide a valid reason, and will be given the option of mailing in their ballots, if circumstances are warranted. Each polling area should have a four man team, comprised equally from members of the two major political parties, and trained in ballot fraud detection.

An individual convicted of ballot fraud should have his lifetime voting rights withdrawn, pay a hefty fine set by Congress, serve community time, and not be allowed to run or participate in any future Federal elections. If a foreign born citizen with naturalization status refuses to participate in the mandated election, and cannot show a reasonable excuse for not voting in two separate elections, then the individual's United States citizenship should be revoked, and the individual returned to the country of his birth.

Individuals who claim voting fraud must be prepared to produce evidence to back their assertions. Making a false statement, whether it be on the internet, broadcasting stations or written should be considered an attack on our democracy, and should be punished by law to the fullest extent. Spreading a lie or false propaganda **knowingly** should not fall under the First Amendment of our Constitution, which guarantees freedom of religion, speech, press and assembly. In 1942, the Supreme Court in Chaplinsky vs. New Hampshire ruled that The First Amendment did not protect "fighting words which, by being said, cause injury or an immediate breach of the peace."

CHAPTER 10

ECONOMIC UPHEAVALS

Economic upheavals have plagued mankind for ever. During the reign of Pharaoh Siptah, archaeological records demonstrate a severe famine. This confirms the Biblical event in the Book of Genesis of how Joseph handled a famine in Egypt, that in actuality encompassed the entire Mediterranean area.

With the advent of trade, economic periods of inflation and recession have been commonly observed. Nineteen major recessions have occurred in the United States since it was founded, and the Federal Government usually finds itself in difficult positions when trying to control economic downturns, known as recessions, or periods of inflation, when items cost more to purchase.

In 1857, embezzlement at the Ohio Life Insurance Company and the sinking of gold being shipped to New York, caused a panic, leading to a recession. The Collapse of the largest U.S. Bank in 1873, led to a run on the money supply and a collapse of the banking system.

The Great Depression of 1929 lasted nine years. One out of four   workers were unemployed at the peak of the economic disruption. Contributing factors were the stock market crash, which ruined businesses and drained life savings. Concurrently the dust bowl drought, in the mid-west, destroyed many farms, adding to the hardships of the time.

The   United   States   experienced many recessions after World War II. In some of these periods, unemployment reached 7 to 8 percent, but, reached eleven percent in the recession of 1980. The actions of the Federal Reserve Bank was the principle cause. In 1979 as it tried to control double digit inflation, the Feds   raised interest rates.   The Iranian oil embargo reduced oil supplies, leading to higher prices, after which the country plunged into a recession.

In April 2020, the American economy lost twenty percent of its jobs. This was a world wide phenomenon, caused mainly by a global Corona virus pandemic, in which not only was jobs lost, but the lives of millions. The estimated monetary global loss was about nine trillions dollars and was the deepest economic downturn since the depression of the thirties.

Within two years, the economy of the United States rebounded as the epidemic subsided and businesses regained momentum. Unemployment levels in America fell to 3.6 % by early 2022. Disruption in the distribution of goods, coupled with the Russo-Ukrainian War put pressure on the American economy, following which, inflationary forces began to take hold.

Inflation is characterized by rise in prices of goods and devaluation of money. The United States has had six inflationary periods since the Second World War, which ended in 1945. Economists mainly use the Consumer Price Index (CPI) and the Personal Consumption Expenditure (PCE) to define the state of the economy. An increase in both indices by 5% defines an inflationary trend.

After World War II, in the Republic of China

under the leadership of Chiang Kai-shek, inflation became so serious and money was so devalued, that a worker had to use a wheel barrel to bring home a weekly salary.

Many times, in the history of humankind, wide spread economic disruption and unrest have been major reasons for governments to fall, prompting a change of rulers and, in some situations, a change in political structure. In Russia, during the first World War, inflation became rampant due to a shortage of workers and basic commodities, leading to widespread famine, and severe inflation. A revolution in 1917, led to the Czar's overthrow, and eventual establishment of Communism.

Greed is another underlying ingredient that feeds on economic disruption. Industries find that the materials that they need in production are more expensive, and they not only pass this increase onto consumers, but the industry adds additional surcharges on its own, to cover potential rise of prices in the future. As an example, a CEO and top executives in a firm whose yearly take home compensation is over 20 million dollars or more, usually would never take a cut in pay and pass the savings onto lowering prices, but instead, the administrative staff of the corporation usually increase their home-take salary. And all along the business chain, this phenomenon occurs, leaving the public with no choice but to deal with inflationary prices.

When the job market needs workers, as exhibited by early months of 2022, the pay for low wage earners are usually raised. The average wage for people that work for large retail corporations, such as Target, Amazon, Best Buy and Lowe's, rose 17% in 2021 to 24,000 dollars; twice the inflationary rate. However, the salary of executives of some of the larger corporations, rose approximately 30% to an average of over ten million. The gap between the pay of executives and workers keeps widening more each year, a very ominous sign.

Greed is noted in most situations of inflation. During the early months of the Russo-Ukrainian War, oil production was reduced. The countries that are oil producers refused to increase production. Scarcity of petroleum fuel forced prices to rise, giving oil producing countries more profit.

During the height of the Covid pandemic, oil consumption declined. The oil companies, to compensate, reduced oil production. At the same time, Russian oil was limited due to the invasion of Ukraine. Crude oil prices jumped to more than a hundred dollars a barrel. While American consumers were paying over five dollars for a gallon of gas, each of the major oil producer companies had had a net profit of six billion. Smaller American oil producers pocketed one to two billion in profit.

But oil producers did not rush to meet the demands of consumers. Before the pandemic of 2021, American oil companies produced approximately thirteen million barrels of oil per day. Presently, in the spring of 2022, the amount of oil produced is slightly more that eleven million barrels a day.

So what are the oil companies doing with their windfall? Are they planning to rapidly increase oil production to meet the demand? Are they using the profits to lower the price of gasoline? Or are they using their added profits to buy back stocks to force the price of of their shares to increase? Most company administrators own large blocks of stock in their corporations, and are given stock options to buy future company stock at a lower option price.

ACUTE PRESCRIPTION
ECONOMIC UPHEAVALS

The Federal government has tools at its disposal to alter economic disruption, such as recession and inflation. Everyone tends to blame the political party in power for the financial difficulty, but the truth is that everyone must take responsibility and do whatever they can to help the economy revive and get back onto a stable tract.

Inflation is defined when prices increase, as measured by the consumer price index (CPI). The CPI calculates the change in prices paid by consumers for services and goods. A recession occurs when the value of goods and services fall and is measured by two consecutive quarters of a negative gross domestic product (GPD), in conjunction with other factors, such as fall in payroll, retail prices, and industrial production. If a recession lasts for a long period of time, the economic down term is referred to as a depression. The two economic states of inflation and recession occasionally occur intertwined.

The Federal Reserve Bank of the federal government has the responsibility of controlling monetary policy. The feat is very difficult as there are many factors that influence the state of the economy. The control of monetary policy is comparable to the control of a cruise ship that weighs over twenty tons, is twenty stories high and is long as four football fields. Maneuverability can be very difficult for the captain of a ship, just like it can be for the Federal Reserve to control the economy. Once forces are moving in one direction, much skill and experience are needed to steer the direction of the economic turmoil.

The federal reserve has powerful tools at its disposal. It enforces governmental financial regulations, clears checks for banks and other depository institutions, controls credit to the banking industry, sets interest on Reserve Balances, as well as other important measures. As a generalization, the Federal Reserve raises interest rates in inflation and lower rates during times of recession.

When interest rates are raised, people tend to spend less, and, theoretically, prices should fall, due to less market demand. On the other hand, in recession, bank rates are lowered, the cost of borrowing money is less expensive, and people are encouraged to borrow and spend more.

The Feds can also increase the cash reserves needed by banks to cover deposits, thus making less cash available in periods of inflation, and visa versa, in periods of recession. The Federal Reserve Board can also change the discount rate on short term loans to the banks, as well as, interest rates on federal bonds.

Inflation is defined as a increase in the price of goods and the concurrent fall in the value of money, resulting in higher cost of an item. Recession, the opposite of Inflation, is a period where the economy contracts, trade and production of goods shrink, unemployment rises, and the value of money increases.

When should the government step in to correct economic disarray? In impending inflation, an increase in the CPI (Consumer

Price Index) of two percent, should alert the Federal Reserve. and in turn, the President and the federal government, to quickly step in to halt the economic turbulence. Interest rates should be raised and other tools should be instituted to lower inflationary forces.

In impending recession, the opposite actions have to be undertaken. A GPD (gross domestic product) negative fall of more than two percent should be a signal to the Federal Reserve to actively use all its available tools to adjust the downfall in the economy. Steps to quickly increase employment and bolster prices should be quickly taken.

The Government must try to keep inflation and recession from getting out of control, but the use of its corrective tools, that were used in the past, operated too slowly, in part because the Federal Reserve appears to change course every three months or longer.

CHRONIC PRESCRIPTION
ECONOMIC UPHEAVALS

The federal reserve should act far quicker to stabilize the economy. Instead of changing interest rates every quarter, the time should be shortened to every two to three weeks. Using computers, economic data should be evaluated at the end of each day, and proper policy moves initiated. The ride may be somewhat bumpy, but the results will keep the country on a more steady course.

Another important suggestion to the chronic prescription, is to make the public aware of the impending economic turbulence, and to request their help to slow the up or down swings of the economy.

In impending inflation, the President should encourage the population not to hoard items that are in short supply, purchase items in quantities that are only necessary, and, ask that wages, rents and prices of goods, voluntarily be kept at the pre-inflationary period. Industry would be encouraged to increase production where indicated and should be requested not to raise prices whenever possible. The Federal reserve would monitor the situation daily and adjust policy as the situation demands.

Very importantly, the populace should be encouraged to avoid panic. The goal of the Federal Reserve is to stabilize prices, while keeping adequate levels of employment. For example, if the price of gasoline is rising too fast because of a period of shortage, the government would ask consumers to voluntarily not completely fill up their car's gas tank, but limit the amount purchased to just what is necessary, for a short period of time, until the situation is under control. The amount of fuel that can be purchased at any one time would be limited.

Businesses requiring gasoline to maintain their services, should be exempt from this voluntary governmental request. Gas producing industries would be voluntarily asked to increase production, and lower the price at the pump, even if the end result is less profits. Government gasoline reserve would be used to increase supply and the federal and state taxes on fuel should be reduced.

Economic up and down swings should be considered national disasters, and, as such, be treated with all the tools that is at the disposal of the leaders of America, and be engaged at as rapid a speed as possible. Everyone must consider that the wide swings in the economy is dangerous for the very existence of the American "way of life" .

Times of economic distress should be treated as if the country is at war. If voluntary requests are not heeded, then Congress should quickly give the executive branch of the government the necessary powers to fight the economic disruption. The President and economic advisers should have to power to demand that industry and American citizens do their shares to achieve economic stability. All parties should work together to effectively arrive at a satisfactory conclusion.

If prices of goods and wages appears to be rising or falling too rapidly, then price stabilization, and limitation of quantities purchased, should be enforced, until the economic situation is under control. In times of recession, factories will not fire anyone, but all, including the CEO's, management and workers will take reduced salaries and work less number of hours per week. A full work schedule will be reinstated when the crisis is over.

Everyone agrees that inflation and recession are definitely detrimental to the health and even survival of the government in control of a nation. The correction of the economic disturbance has to be swift and effective, and lead to a soft landing in economic swings, so that the economy quickly evens out, without surging too far in either direction.

The people who are usually hurt the most during economic upheavals are the majority of those who are the lowest wage earners. With inflation, money buys less, and during depression, this group is the first to lose their jobs, find themselves unable to pay rent or mortgages, lose their health benefits if they become unemployed, and find themselves, homeless. On the other hand, the wealthy just rides out the economic turmoil.

In the Great Depression of the nineteen thirties, 25% of the nation's total work force lost their jobs. Close to thirteen million workers had no employment. Wages of those 75% who were able to keep a job fell 43%. One of the factors of causation was the inadequate response of the Federal Reserve. The depression lasted ten years. The programs of the New Deal and World War II contributed to end the depression.

Irrespective of the economic situation, a just

society should ensure that all its members have the basic needs of shelter, food, clothing, and medical care. No one should have to experience homelessness, hunger or unaffordable medical care, especially in America, one of the richest country in the history of humankind.

CHAPTER 11

STUDENT LOANS

In 1965, the federal government introduced a guaranteed student loan program. Lending money to poorer Americans to obtain a college education is certainly a good investment, considering that educated students of today will be the future leaders of the country.

At the onset, direct loans were capitalized using United States Bonds, and later changed to be directly issued by the Department of Energy. Students, who borrow to pay for schooling, are obligated to pay back the principle and accumulated interest. The interest rates of governmental loans are usually lower when compared to private student loans.

The federal student loan interest rate depends on the loan type and the date that the loan is issued. Between July 1, 2022 and June 30, 2023, the fixed interest rate on a direct subsidized loan given to an undergraduate is 4.99%, an unsubsidized loan to a graduate, 6.54%, and 7.54% for a direct loan to professional students.

Forty five million Americans are responsible to pay back student loans. Twenty percent are over the age of fifty. Four years after leaving college, one out of every two black students, who obtained a student loan, still owes more than their original loan, as compared to one in five of white debtors. Unlike most other loans, a student loan is not subject to bankruptcy laws, and must be repaid. Elderly individuals who have not paid off their student loans, have had their social security checks garnished.

During the presidency of Barack Obama, outstanding student loans reached one trillion dollars. Borrowers were given the option of paying off their loans with monthly amounts that are proportionate to the total amount of their salary, rather than the previous method of collecting a fixed sum every month. A problem with this repayment method is that by paying lower premiums, the time of the loan is extended, increasing the amount of interest that has to be repaid. The banks and loan services that give loans are guaranteed to be repaid by the federal government. At the present time, the Department of Education has loaned 1.6 trillion dollars to students.

The federally guaranteed program ended the last day in June, 2010, but many are still paying the outstanding loan in 2022. Presently, banks and other lending institutions provide the monies for loans to students. These loans are guaranteed by the federal government, and if a student borrower defaults, the Department of Education pays the lending bank 97% of the principle balance. Even though the government takes over the loan, the ex-student borrower is still obligated to pay back the remainder of the loan to the federal government.

Added to the confusion, there are many different types of student loans and payment options. A defaulted loan is farmed out by the government to a collection agency, that takes on the responsibility to obtain what is still owed.

Students assume that they will be able to obtain a good paying job after they graduate from college or graduate school. However, this generalization was applicable in the past, but may not be apply to today's economic situation.

ACUTE PRESCRIPTION
COLLEGE STUDENT LOANS

The young people of America are the most valuable resources that the country has. In time, they will be responsible for leading the nation, and taking over the reigns of government, industry, social services, and the sciences.

Huge debt from outstanding student loans have hindered the borrowing generation from providing their families with the standard of living that their non-borrower counterparts enjoy. Many young families desire a home of their own and other economic benefits, but find their dreams are not attainable, due to the burden of debt that they assumed, in order to become educated.

What should be done immediately to alleviate the burden of student debt loan? One solution is to wipe their loan out completely, but, even though this is an ideal solution, congress would never agree. The other alternative is to forgo any future interest that is due and just require that the remainder of the original loan be paid off; amortized at payments based on current yearly salary of the debtor. After ten years, all monies owned will be forgiven and no further payments will be due.

CHRONIC PRESCRIPTION
COLLEGE STUDENT LOANS

Higher education in State Universities and Colleges should be free, for families whose yearly income is less than $50,000. The student would be required to be employed by the school for a minimum of six hours a week to pay for room and board. Above a yearly family salary of $50,000 level, tuition would be based on a sliding scale. Above $100,000 in family yearly salary, the student would pay full state school tuition. Students that require a loan would be entitled to obtain student scholarships. A student with free tuition who was the recipient of a fiscal award must donate the proceeds to the attending college.

Simple interest rates would be set at 2%. Payback can be initiated any time after graduation, but, if requested to be delayed, must begin three years after obtaining a diploma. Payback of a loan at any time will incur no penalty.

The amount in monthly payments would depend on the size of the loan, and the yearly salary of the individual. Like current loan requirements, a student loan cannot be resolved through bankruptcy. Students that drop out of college will be expected to pay back the amount loaned, starting no later than three years after leaving the academic environment.

Private colleges would be encouraged to admit students from low income families, supplementing the tuition through scholarships and work programs. Student loans would be available at the same terms that applies to students attending state colleges.

If Social and Emotional Learning Programs (Mastering Life's Skills) are available to students in lower and upper school grades, then upon entering college and graduate school, these students will have adequate knowledge of how to handle their financial needs.

CHAPTER 12

RESPONSIBILTY OF CITIZENSHIP

The question is constantly being battered around as to who is responsible for a particular set of decisions. Unfortunately, when problems arise, everybody tends to blame someone else. No one wants to be held responsible and tries to cast it onto another individual. President Harry Truman adorned his desk with the popular adage, "The Buck Stops Here."

In the mid 1890's, during the era of the Third French Republic, a Jewish army captain, Alfred Dreyfus was convicted of treason, being accused of giving top secrets to the Germans. Anti-Semitic groups, including leading newspapers and prominent individuals fostered this untruth, leading to Dreyfus's conviction. A journalist, Emile Zola, attacked the French Army's position of lies and, with popular support, Dreyfus was released from prison. The Army did not officially admit to his innocence until 1995. Who was to blame for this charade? The

French military were the main culprits, but all who supported the falsehood have to share the blame in the fabrication of the facts.

The My Lai incident in the Viet Nam War was a massacre by American army personnel against unarmed Vietnamese civilians. In 1968, all 500 residents, including the elderly and children, of the village of My Lei were brutally killed, and some of females were raped. The village was burnt to the ground, and the livestock slaughtered. The incident was covered-up for almost a year, when it was exposed by the American free press.

The army brass that were involved tried to down play the incident until a soldier, not involved in the incident, brought it to the attention of President and the Pentagon. Fourteen soldiers were held responsible and tried in court for the massacre. The lieutenant in charge received a life sentence, but only had to serve ten years.

Adolf Hitler, the leader of the Third Reich was able to convince the majority of Germans and many other anti-Semitic European nations to perform ethnic genocide on six million Jews, as well as a small group of other "undesirable" individuals.

In 1938, President Roosevelt convened the Evian Conference in France; the main purpose to encourage countries to accept more Jewish refugees into their countries, even though, the United States had a very restrictive quota of the number of Jews it would admit. Roosevelt did nor personally attend the meeting, but sent a business man as his representative.

Thirty two countries participated in the conference. Only the Dominican Republic volunteered to take some of the Jewish refugees, but none of the other nations would agree to receive any. The Soviet Union not only refused to admit Jews, but declared that anyone crossing the Soviet border would be shot as a spy.

The Nazi regime and collaborators slaughtered many Jews throughout Europe. Other Jews were placed in concentration camps, where many were killed in gas chambers. The bodies were burnt in ovens or interred in mass graves. The smell of burning flesh permeated Europe. The policies of Hitler gave impetus to increasing overt antisemitism not only in Germany, but spread to France, Hungary and other European countries.

Who should take the blame for such a disaster? Yes, Hitler and his henchmen must be given the major share of responsibility for the mass slaughter, but as in most situations, all individuals that participated in Nazi policies must likewise assume blame.

On November 9th and the following day, Nazi henchmen and ordinary German citizens torched synagogues, vandalized Jewish business and homes, and arrested 30,000 innocent Jewish men. The event is known as Kristallnacht, the "Night of Broken Glass". Most Germans who witnessed the attacks, stood by and cheered. Every German, even if they passively witnessed the event, has to assume responsibility for the wrong that was done. Following the war, the Government of Germany made restitution for the Nazi wrongdoings.

Recently, on January 6, 2021, in America, an insurrection was carried out on the steps of the Capital building in Washington, D.C., which houses both chambers of Congress. A group of non-law abiding individuals stormed the sacred governmental building, killing and scathing guards, who were trying to halt the group from entering. "Kill the Vice President" was the cry heard from the violent mob, as they waved signs of support for the presiding President.   A Congressional Committee is presently investigating who is responsible.

Many Americans, who refuse to accept official unbiased findings of the congressional committee, who continue to make unsubstantial excuses, and who insist on promoting false claims, are just as responsible for the insurrection as those who were physically involved in the treasonable event.

What is the responsibility of a citizen who observes an act that is unpatriotic, prejudicial, or unfairly harmful to others? Saying nothing and walking away is condoning the nefarious behavior.

Americans still have the power of free speech. "If You see something, say something".   Don't idly sit by. Write and visit your Congressperson. March in a parade opposing the act. Be active and let your voice by heard.

CHAPTER 13

EVALUATING THE TRUTH

Too many Americans tend to believe false propaganda that they hear from biased sources, such as radio, television, printed materials or internet. Many of these individuals are very intelligent, but are willing to accept lies, if the concepts coincides with their fundamental beliefs, or they actually think that the false statements are absolutely true.

As an example, one political party has been expounding the concept that the 2020 election for President was rigged, and that the voting was not counted correctly. In spite of the fact that many courts, and numerous recounts of votes in many states by impartial participants have found that there was no fraud, the proponents of the lie continually keep swearing to its validity, even though no documented proof can substantiate the claim.

A far-right conspiracy theorist used his Infowars media company to spread vicious lies about students that were murdered in the Sandy Hook school shooting. He was convicted for defaming the families of the victims, and is liable for over $4 million.

CHRONIC PRESCRIPTION
EVALUATING THE TRUTH

Americans should be given the tools to be able to discern what statements are false and what are true. They must be made aware of the benefits of the American Republic, as well as to its limitations, of which citizens must try to change for the betterment of its citizenry; the country that their children will inherit.

How does one accomplish these goals? The answer depends on the willingness of America to insist of adding a Life Management Skill Program, (aka, Social and Emotional Learning Program), to the curriculum of our school systems, as discussed in Chapter 3. Teaching children how to identify truth from fiction, as well as emphasizing good citizenship are very important subjects, which are easily handled by school discussion groups.

CHAPTER 14

THE GREATNESS OF AMERICA

The type of government that the founding fathers of the United States envisioned had never existed before in prior history They felt that most men were created equal and that this select group should enjoy a government that is free from monarchical and despotic rule. Their blueprint was based on their classical schooling in antiquity and the favorable, as well as, unfavorable aspects of the government of England.

Their role models were Plato's vision of a "perfect" government , which was designed by his mentor and teacher, Socrates, as well as, those parts of English Law, that they felt were suitable. They fostered the concept of liberty, free speech, freedom of religion, due process of law and the ability for the founding group to express ideas in lawful assembly. However, The Constitution that was finally adopted did not apply to the majority of women, children or African American slaves.

Not everyone had the right to vote in the newly established country. All under 21 years of age, slaves, women, most Jews and Catholics, as well as non-land owners were eliminated. Only twenty percent of the population was eligible to vote.

At first, voting was done by a show of hands, and gradually changed to secret paper ballots. At the onset, some of the colonies published a list of how each person voted. Voting fraud was not uncommon. Some individuals were paid to vote for a particular candidate. The right to vote required ownership of property. It was not uncommon that citizens who had no land were handed phony deeds of plots of land, so they were able to cast a vote. Naturally, corrupt voters were told how to vote, and were financially compensated. After the election, phony deeds were destroyed. Some elected officials were corrupt and many qualified voters were denied the ability to submit a ballot. Bribing to have an individual change the vote was not uncommon. Some ballots were lost, destroyed or miscounted.

States were given the power to determine who was eligible to vote. Reform of many voting irregularities in Federal elections were gradually instituted, and, over time, most citizens were given the privilege to be able to vote, without having to pass religious or literacy tests. States determine the eligibility to vote, and regulations varies from state to state. In general, non-citizens, felons, and some mentally incapacitated individuals do not have voting privileges.

The first New Jersey constitution, adopted in July 2, 1776, stated that "all inhabitants" had the right to vote if an individual owned land worth more than fifty English pounds. Married women were excluded since their husbands owned the property. Much debate over women's suffrage ensued. Debates were contentious. The words "all inhabitants" excluded slaves, children, foreigners and was eventually extended to include women. In 1807, the New Jersey all male legislature took away the women's right to vote.

Fortunately, the Founding Fathers of America, implanted within The Constitution, an ability for future generations to update the original document. Article V of the Constitution provides that a two thirds majority in both the House of Representative and the Senate, or by a constitutional convention called by a two thirds of the State legislatures, has the ability to amend the original document. The President was not allowed to have input in accepting a new amendment. Factually, none of the twenty seven amendments that were eventually added, was approved by a constitutional convention.

After the Civil War, universal male suffrage was adopted, which included freed black male slaves. Women were not permitted to vote until 1920 with the passage of the 19th Amendment. But many states controlled voting by gerrymandering, charging a voting tax, or requiring comprehensive reading and writing tests, that had to be passed in order to vote.   The 24th Amendment of 1964 prohibited denying voting privileges because of refusal to pay a tax in Federal elections and in 1971, the voting age was lowered to 18 years of age from 21.

In 2021, election fraud was attempted by a minority group of individuals who tried to get control of this great nation. They tried to overturn the 2020 presidential election by claiming voting irregularities, supposedly, designed by the opposing political party, and did their best to intimidate voter officials.

False statements claimed that their leader was the "legitimate President" and that the newly elected President of the United States, should not be confirmed. They sought to obtain their goals by intimidation, bribing and insurrection. As previously mentioned, on January 6, 2021, a mob who supported the outgoing sitting President, stormed the Capital Building, threatened the life of the Vice President, and tried to prevent Congress from approving the peaceful transfer of power of the Oval Office, as directed by the U.S. Constitution.

Numerous recounts of votes in many States, as well as numerous court cases could not find any evidence of voter fraud. Even though the proponents of fraudulent voting, could not prove their false claims, they continue to foster this big lie. In truth, a handful of cases of voter fraud reached notoriety; however, most, if not all, were committed by members of the group claiming voter fraud.

Polarization has weakened America. Political lying has weakened America. Politicians take an oath to protect the Constitution and the Country, and yet, many put the selfish agenda of their political party above the good of the

Country, and do not honor their pledges of allegiance.

But in spite of the fact that some politicians bend the truth to suit their needs, America is still one of the best countries in which to live. The pendulum between the conservative right and the liberal left will continually swing back and forth, depending who is in control. Hopefully, policies in the middle will prevail. Compromise is the only hope we have, if America is to survive.

The greatness of America is its acceptance of peoples of all race, religion and sexual preference. Unfortunately, much pressure to take these freedoms away is being fostered by a fringe group of individuals. They want to take away the vote and other privileges from many of those of color and underprivileged. This conservative group uses tricks like gerrymandering, eliminating convenient voting places, demanding proof of residency, as well as other measures to prevent voting. Fortunately, forces of democracy are constantly pushing back on efforts to take away minority citizen's rights.

At the present time, individuals favoring

autocracy, that is a system of government in which one individual has absolute power, appears to be rising throughout the world. Countries, such as Russia, Saudi Arabia, North Korea are autocratic, and many other countries appear to be going in that direction. The change from a democratic to an autocratic government can be very subtle, and citizens, who support the change, are not usually aware that they are slowly giving up their democratic privileges. The Nazi takeover of Germany in the early 1930's is a perfect example. Some Jewish groups actually favored the rise of Hitler at the onset of his term in office, only to find themselves the victims of his evil policies. In 2022, 94.6% of Tunisians approved a new constitution which approved a one man rule. The previous democratic government in Tunisia had failed to provide jobs and eliminate widespread corruption. The new autocratic constitution of Tunisia weakens the power of Parliament, gives its new President the ability to appoint government ministers and judges, and to institute laws.

The United States must be careful not to follow the path that Tunisia has taken. America can overcome the problems that it faces. The Country was able to separate from an unjust monarchy, overcome a civil war, throw off the yoke of slavery, fight many international wars, survive numerous economic upheavals and still survive. At the present time, many conservative groups want to turn back the clock and establish a nation which they alone control. Discrimination and bigotry is ever increasing, and the rights of many groups that were taken for granted are slowly being eroded and, in many cases, have been withdrawn.

In America, a minority group of individuals appear to be trying to kidnap the country. The legislatures and the courts are swinging toward the extreme right. This is an a classic example of an early phase of how a republic gradually converts into an autocratic state, a very ominous sign.

Many nations have come and gone. The Pharaohs of Egypt, the city states of Ancient Greece, the almighty Roman Empire, the Absolute Authority of Kings, Emperors, and Czars, as well as, Dictatorships, such as Nazi Germany and Stalin's Russia, have all disappeared.

Only time will reveal the fate of America.

Why is instructing our children to know how to handle possible future situations of danger, proper ways to handle relationships, and instilling knowledge of patriotism important? Statistics of American problems indicate that something must be done.

Every year in America, twenty one million suffer with the addiction of alcohol and drug abuse, twenty percent of students are subjected to being bullied, eighty thousand teenage females become pregnant, twenty percent of women experience completed or attempted rape, fifty percent of marriages end in divorce, eighty percent of Americans experience emotional abuse, at least one time in their lives, prejudice is widespread, and the list of other harmful behavior is endless. In addition, we are not instilling in America the benefits that a republic offers, and what our citizens would face if an autocratic regime would replace our current system of government.

This is the reason that a teaching program similar to Managing Life's Skills (aka, Social and Emotional Learning), as documented in Chapter 2 of this book, is so important. The only possibility of counteracting the harmful direction that America appears to be heading, is to instill in our youth, solutions of how to avoid harm and how to handle situations, that they might be exposed to during their lifetime.

Yes, instilling proper and fundamental values of fairness and good citizenship into the majority of Americans may take many years, but the sooner we begin to incorporate a program, similar to "Mastering Life Skills (Social and Emotional Learning) into our school system to educate our young people, the sooner the country has the possibility of achieving the goals of being an harmonious and just.

ABOUT THE AUTHOR

Melvin S. Rosh, M.D. is a retired physician, who practiced Pediatrics and Pediatric Allergy for a half a century. After retiring from practice, he donated time to a local municipal hospital, responsible for the care of indigent children.

Dr. Rosh is the founder and CEO of a non-profit corporation, Rewarding Life, Inc., whose mission is to instruct children how to vicariously avoid and handle harmful situations in the future, such as drug addiction, prejudice, discrimination, and sexual molestation, as well as, give them knowledge of life mastering skills.

He has written several books, as well as professional and lay articles. A list of some of his publications are as follows. All books can be purchased at fine bookstores and the Amazon website. All royalties are donated to the non- profit corporation, Rewarding Life, Inc.

BOOKS BY MELVIN S. ROSH, M.D.

A Rewarding Life
Preparing Children for the Future
Role of Schools in Educating Children in
Life Mastering Skills
The Autobiography of Dr. Mel
Divine Energy
The Guest Who Came from Nowhere
El Invitado Que Vino de la Nada
A Medical Doc's Prescription for Healing
an Ailing America
Healing an Ailing United States Federal
Government.